YOU'RE
THE CHEF

SUPER
Pasta AND Rice
DISHES

Jennifer S. Larson Photographs by **Brie Cohen**

M MILLBROOK PRESS • MINNEAPOLIS

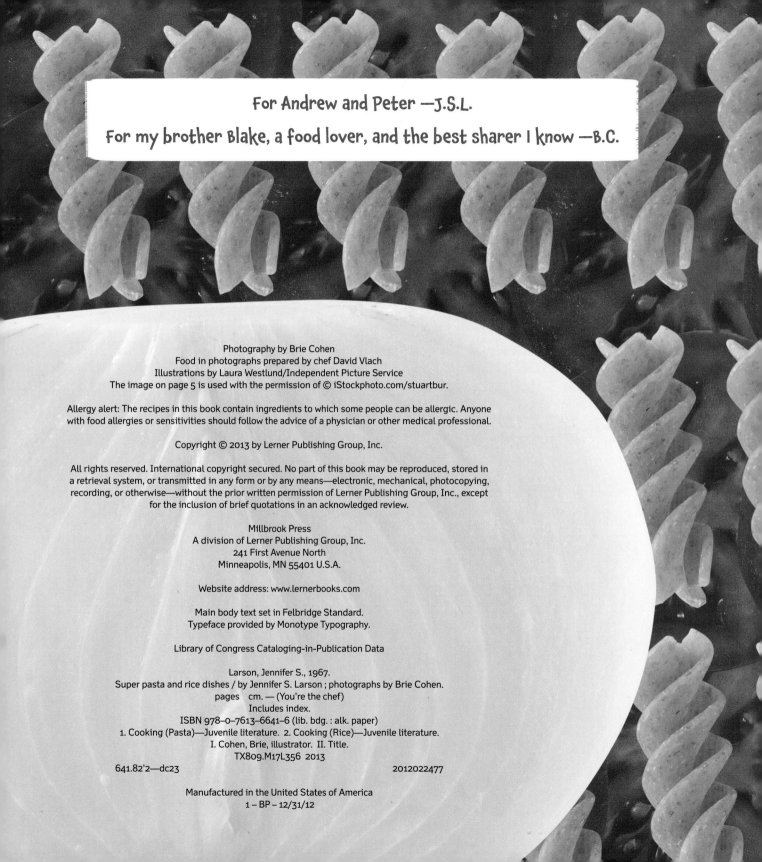

For Andrew and Peter —J.S.L.

For my brother Blake, a food lover, and the best sharer I know —B.C.

Photography by Brie Cohen
Food in photographs prepared by chef David Vlach
Illustrations by Laura Westlund/Independent Picture Service
The image on page 5 is used with the permission of © iStockphoto.com/stuartbur.

Allergy alert: The recipes in this book contain ingredients to which some people can be allergic. Anyone with food allergies or sensitivities should follow the advice of a physician or other medical professional.

Millbrook Press
A division of Lerner Publishing Group, Inc.
241 First Avenue North
Minneapolis, MN 55401 U.S.A.

Website address: www.lernerbooks.com

Main body text set in Felbridge Standard.
Typeface provided by Monotype Typography.

Library of Congress Cataloging-in-Publication Data

Larson, Jennifer S., 1967.
Super pasta and rice dishes / by Jennifer S. Larson ; photographs by Brie Cohen.
pages   cm. — (You're the chef)
Includes index.
ISBN 978–0–7613–6641–6 (lib. bdg. : alk. paper)
1. Cooking (Pasta)—Juvenile literature. 2. Cooking (Rice)—Juvenile literature.
I. Cohen, Brie, illustrator. II. Title.
TX809.M17L356 2013
641.82'2—dc23   2012022477

Manufactured in the United States of America
1 – BP – 12/31/12

TABLE OF CONTENTS

Mmmm. Are you hungry for some tasty and filling rice and pasta dishes? YOU can be the chef and make food for yourself and your family. Follow these recipes, and surprise your family with some delicious meals!

I developed these recipes with the help of my kids, who are seven and ten years old. They can't do all the cooking on their own yet, but they can do a lot.

Can't get enough of cooking? Check out www.lerneresource.com for bonus recipes, healthful eating tips, links to cooking technique videos, metric conversions, and more!

BEFORE YOU START

Reserve your space! Always ask for permission to work in the kitchen.

Find a helper! You will need an adult helper for some tasks. Talk with this person to decide what steps you can do on your own and what steps the adult will help with.

Make a plan! Read through the whole recipe before you start cooking. Do you have the ingredients you'll need? If you don't know what a certain ingredient is, see page 31 to find out more. Do you understand each step? If you don't understand a technique, such as *simmer* or *slice*, turn to page 7. At the beginning of each recipe, you'll see how much time you'll need to prepare the recipe and to cook it. The recipe will also tell you how many servings it makes. Small drawings at the top of each recipe let you know what major kitchen equipment you'll need—such as a stovetop, a blender, or a microwave.

stovetop

blender

knife

microwave

oven

Wash up! Always wash your hands with soap and water before you start cooking. And wash them again after you touch raw eggs, meat, or fish.

Get it together! Find the tools you'll use, such as measuring cups or a mixing bowl. Gather all the ingredients you'll need. That way you won't have to stop to look for things once you start cooking.

SAFETY TIPS

That's sharp! Your adult helper needs to be in the kitchen when you are using a knife, a grater, or a peeler. If you are doing the cutting, use a cutting board. Cut away from your body, and keep your fingers away from the blade.

That's hot! Be sure an adult is in the kitchen if you use the stove or the oven. Your adult helper can help you cook on the stove and take hot things out of the oven.

Tie it back! If you have long hair, tie it back or wear a hat. If you have long sleeves, roll them up. You want to keep your hair and clothing out of the food and away from flames or other heat sources.

Turn that handle! When cooking on the stove, turn the pot handle toward the back. That way, no one will accidentally bump the pot and knock it off the stove.

Wash it! If you are working with raw eggs or meat, you need to keep things extra clean. After cutting raw meat or fish, wash the knife and the cutting board right away. They must be clean before you use them to cut anything else.

Go slowly! Take your time when you're working. When you are doing something for the first time, such as peeling or grating, be sure not to rush.

Finish the job right!

One of your most important jobs as a chef is to clean up when you're done. Wash the dishes with soap and warm water. Wipe off the countertop or the table. Put away any unused ingredients. The adults in your house will be more excited for you to cook next time if you take charge of cleaning up.

Above all, have fun!

COOKING TOOLS

baking pans

bowls

can opener

colander

cutting board

dry measuring cups

fork

frying pan

grater

knives

large spoon

liquid measuring cup

measuring spoons

oven mitt

pie pan

saucepans

serrated knife

spatula

tongs

whisk

wooden spoon

TECHNIQUES

bake: to cook in the oven

boil: to heat liquid on a stovetop until the liquid starts to bubble

chop: to cut food into small pieces using a knife

cover: to put a lid on a pan or pot containing food

discard: to throw away or put in a compost bin. Discarded parts of fruits and vegetables and eggshells can be put in a compost bin, if you have one.

drain: to pour the liquid off a food. You can drain food by pouring it into a colander or strainer. If you are draining water or juice from canned food, you can also use the lid to hold the food back while the liquid pours out.

grate: to use a food grater to shred food into small pieces

grease: to coat a pan in oil or butter so baked food won't stick to the bottom

mix: to stir food using a spoon or fork

preheat: to turn the oven to the temperature you will need for baking. An oven takes about 15 minutes to heat up.

serrated: a tool, such as a knife, that has a bumpy edge

set aside: to put nearby in a bowl or plate or on a clean work space

simmer: to boil at a low heat setting. The liquid will be boiling with very tiny bubbles.

slice: to cut food into thin pieces

sprinkle: to scatter on top

whisk: to stir quickly with a fork or whisk

MEASURING

To measure **dry ingredients**, such as sugar or flour, spoon the ingredient into a measuring cup until it is full. Then use the back of a table knife to level it off. Do not pack it down unless the recipe tells you to. Do not use measuring cups made for liquids.

When you're measuring a **liquid**, such as milk or water, use a clear glass or plastic measuring cup. Set the cup on the table or a counter and pour the liquid into the cup. Pour slowly and stop when the liquid has reached the correct line.

Don't measure your ingredients over the bowl they will go into. If you accidentally spill, you might have way too much!

serves 6

preparation time: 30 minutes
baking time: 30 minutes

ingredients:

4 tablespoons unsalted butter
2 medium carrots
8 ounces (2 cups) cheddar cheese
8 cups water
8 ounces (2 cups) whole wheat
   macaroni
2 tablespoons flour
1 teaspoon dry mustard
2 cups low-fat milk
½ teaspoon salt
pepper
3 tablespoons whole wheat bread
   crumbs

equipment:

2-quart baking pan
paper towel
grater
measuring cup—1 cup
medium-large saucepan
colander
small saucepan
measuring spoons
wooden spoon
liquid measuring cup
whisk
small microwave-safe bowl
oven mitts

Magnificent Macaroni and Cheese

Have you ever made macaroni and cheese from scratch? Now's your chance. Serve it with a salad or a vegetable on the side for a healthy meal.

1. **Preheat** the oven to 350°F.

2. **Grease** a baking pan with 1 tablespoon butter. You can use a paper towel to rub the butter on the bottom and sides of the pan.

3. **Wash** the carrots under cool water. **Grate** the carrots using the grater. Discard the stems. Grate enough to measure about 1 cup.

4. **Wash** and dry the grater. Use it to **grate** the cheese.

5. **Place** a medium-large saucepan on the stove. **Add** 8 cups water. Turn the burner under the saucepan on high. When the water boils, **add** the macaroni. Cook for 8 to 10 minutes, or follow the directions on the package.

6. When the noodles are done cooking, ask an adult to **drain** them into a colander in the sink. Run the noodles under cold water. **Pour** the macaroni back into the saucepan.

Turn the page for more Magnificent Macaroni and Cheese

7. **Place** a small saucepan on the stove. **Add** 2 tablespoons of butter. **Turn** the burner under the saucepan on medium. **Melt** the butter. **Add** the flour and dry mustard. **Stir** with a whisk or wooden spoon until well mixed. Slowly **add** half the milk. Stir with a whisk until there are no lumps. Add the rest of the milk and stir. Continue to stir every couple of minutes until the mixture starts to boil and thicken. Turn off heat. **Add** salt and pepper. **Whisk** until well mixed.

8. **Add** the grated carrots to the macaroni. **Stir**. **Add** the milk sauce and **stir** well. **Add** the grated cheese. **Mix** with the wooden spoon until the clumps of cheese are mixed in. **Scoop** the macaroni mixture into the greased baking pan.

9. **Place** 1 tablespoon of butter in a microwave-safe bowl. Cook on high in the microwave for 30 seconds, or until butter is melted. Use oven mitts to take out the bowl. **Add** the bread crumbs and stir. **Sprinkle** the buttery bread crumbs on top of the macaroni.

10. Use oven mitts to **place** the baking pan in the oven. **Bake** for 30 minutes, or until lightly brown on top. Use oven mitts to take the pan out of the oven. Let sit for 10 minutes and serve.

Tasty Pad Thai Noodles

You'll love the sweet, zingy flavor of these noodles. This recipe is inspired by the food of Thailand, a country in Asia.

1. **Crack** the eggs into a small bowl. **Whisk** the eggs with a fork or a whisk.

Turn the page for more Tasty Pad Thai Noodles

preparation time: 35 minutes
cooking time: 15 minutes

ingredients:
3 eggs
¾ cup unsalted peanuts
3 to 4 green onions
2 small limes (or 3 tablespoons bottled lime juice)
3 tablespoons ketchup
1 tablespoon brown sugar
¼ cup soy sauce
8 cups water
2 cups bean sprouts (also called mung bean sprouts)
6 ounces flat rice noodles (or a flour pasta, such as linguine)
3 tablespoons vegetable oil
½ teaspoon garlic powder
8-ounce bag of shredded carrots (2 cups)

equipment:
4 small bowls
fork or whisk
knife
cutting board
measuring spoons
measuring cups—
¼ cup, ½ cup
spoon
large saucepan
liquid measuring cup
colander or strainer
large frying pan
spatula
tongs or 2 wooden spoons

Tasty Pad Thai Noodles continued

2. Use a knife and cutting board to **chop** the peanuts into pieces. Set aside in a small bowl.

3. **Wash** the green onions under cool water. Next, use the knife and cutting board to **cut** off the roots and discard. Remove any dry or wilted green parts. Then **slice** the onions into small pieces about ½ inch long. You can use both the white and green parts of the onion. Cut enough to measure about ½ cup. Set aside.

4. On the cutting board, **cut** a lime in half. **Squeeze** half the lime into a small bowl to get the juice out. You will need to **scoop** out the seeds with a small spoon. Repeat with the other half. Then do the same with the second lime. **Measure** 3 tablespoons of lime juice into another small bowl and set aside.

TRY THIS!

If you like, add 8 ounces of chicken or firm **tofu** to this recipe. Before cooking the chicken or tofu, cut it into bite-sized chunks. Then cook in 2 tablespoons vegetable oil in the frying pan before you cook the other ingredients. The chicken should be cooked all the way through. The tofu should be lightly browned on all sides. Set aside and then add to the frying pan in step 11.

5. In a small bowl, **add** the lime juice, ketchup, brown sugar, and soy sauce. **Mix** well with a spoon.

6. **Put** water in a saucepan. Turn the burner under the saucepan on high and **cover** the pan. Bring to a boil.

7. Place bean sprouts in a colander or a strainer and **rinse** in the sink under cool water. Keep the sprouts in the colander, and ask an adult to **dip** them in the boiling water for 30 seconds. Run the sprouts under cool water again. Then take them out of the colander and set them aside.

8. **Place** the rice noodles in the boiling water. Cook for 3 to 5 minutes (or follow the directions on the package). When the noodles are done cooking, ask an adult to **drain** them into the colander in the sink. Run the noodles under cold water. Set aside.

9. **Pour** the vegetable oil in a frying pan. Turn the burner under the pan on medium-high. **Add** the garlic and the shredded carrots. Cook for 2 minutes, stirring with a spatula. **Move** the carrots to the edge and clear a spot in the middle.

10. **Pour** the eggs into the middle of the pan. Let them cook for about 30 seconds until they begin to set. Then use the spatula to **stir** the eggs and **flip** them over. Keep stirring and flipping the eggs until they are cooked on all sides. They should be firm, not wet or gooey.

11. **Pour** in the lime sauce and mix it together with the eggs and carrots. **Add** the noodles and bean sprouts. **Stir**. (This can be tricky. Try using tongs or 2 wooden spoons to toss the ingredients together.) **Add** the peanuts and green onions. **Stir** everything together. Turn off the burner and serve.

serves: 4

preparation time: 30 minutes
cooking time: 20 minutes

ingredients:

8 cups water
8 ounces (2 cups) pasta in the
   shape of your choice, such
   as shells, bow ties, or penne
½ red or green pepper
1 small tomato
2 green onions
1 large carrot
½ cup frozen corn
½ cup raisins
¼ cup sunflower seeds
¼ cup salad dressing: ranch,
   Italian, or other favorites

equipment:

large saucepan
liquid measuring cup
colander
large bowl
measuring spoons
wooden spoon
knife
cutting board
5 small bowls
serrated knife
grater
microwave-safe bowl
oven mitts
large spoon
4 bowls for serving

Party Pasta Salad

It's a party in a bowl!
In this recipe, everyone gets to put his or her own toppings
on a bowl of pasta salad. What toppings will you try?

1. **Fill** a saucepan with water and place it on the
   stove. **Cover**, and turn the burner under the pan on
   high. Heat water until boiling, and **add** pasta. Cook
   according to the directions on the package.

2. When the pasta is done, ask an adult
   to **drain** it into a colander in the sink.
   Run the noodles under cold water.
   Pour the pasta in a large bowl. **Add**
   the vegetable oil to the pasta and
   mix with a wooden spoon. The oil will
   help keep the noodles from sticking
   together.

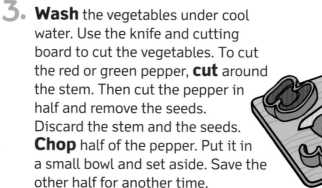

3. **Wash** the vegetables under cool
   water. Use the knife and cutting
   board to cut the vegetables. To cut
   the red or green pepper, **cut** around
   the stem. Then cut the pepper in
   half and remove the seeds.
   Discard the stem and the seeds.
   Chop half of the pepper. Put it in
   a small bowl and set aside. Save the
   other half for another time.

14

4. To cut the tomato, it works best to use a serrated knife, a knife with bumps along the sharp edge. First, **cut** out the green or brown circle on the top. Discard it. Then **chop** the rest of the tomato. Put it in a small bowl and set aside.

Turn the page for more Party Pasta Salad

TRY THIS!

Get creative with your toppings. Some other ingredients to try are olives, pepperoni, broccoli, dried cranberries, cooked chicken pieces, fresh herbs, or chopped walnuts. What else can you think of?

5. To cut the green onions, **cut** off the roots and discard. Remove any dry or wilted green parts. Then **slice** the onions into small pieces about ½ inch long. You can use both the white and green parts of the onion. Put it in a small bowl and set aside.

6. Use a grater to **grate** the carrots into a small bowl. Discard the stem.

7. **Measure** the frozen corn into a small microwave-safe bowl. Cook for 1 minute, or until corn is not frozen. It does not need to be cooked, just thawed. Use oven mitts to **remove** the bowl from the microwave.

8. **Measure** the raisins and sunflower seeds into a small bowl.

9. Use a large spoon to **scoop** the pasta into 4 bowls, 1 for each person. Let everyone choose his or her own toppings to **sprinkle** on the pasta. Then **top** with a favorite salad dressing.

Do you have a garden?

If you do, you could try growing some fresh herbs, like basil, chives, oregano, or parsley. Fresh herbs make this recipe—and many others—extra yummy. Even if you don't have space for a garden, you can grow herbs in a pot outside or by a sunny window inside. Then, when you're cooking, pluck a few leaves from an herb. Chop them up, and add some zest to almost any meal!

Spaghetti Pie

Have some pie for dinner! This hearty dish uses spaghetti for the piecrust.

1. **Preheat** the oven to 350°F.

2. **Grease** the bottom and sides of a pie pan with 1 tablespoon butter. You can use a paper towel to rub the butter into the pan.

3. **Wash** the green pepper under cool water. Use the knife and the cutting board to **cut** around the stem of the green pepper. Then cut the green pepper in half and remove the seeds. Discard the stem and the seeds. **Chop** the rest of the green pepper. Set aside.

Turn the page for more Spaghetti Pie

serves 6

preparation time: 45 minutes
cooking time: 30 minutes

ingredients:
2 tablespoons butter
1 small green pepper
1 small onion
2 eggs
2 ounces (½ cup) mozzarella cheese
1 tablespoon vegetable oil
½ teaspoon garlic powder
1 pound (16 ounces) ground beef or turkey
2 cups pasta sauce
8 cups water
1 6-ounce package whole wheat spaghetti
⅓ cup Parmesan cheese
1 cup ricotta cheese

equipment:
9-inch pie pan
paper towel
knife
cutting board
2 small bowls
fork
grater
large frying pan
measuring spoons
spatula
measuring cups—
⅓ cup, ½ cup, 1 cup
liquid measuring cup
large saucepan
colander
large bowl
large spoon
spoon
oven mitts

17

4. **Cut** off both ends of the onion. Set the onion on one of the flat parts you made by cutting it. Cut the onion in half. **Peel** off and discard the papery layers around the outside. Lay the onion half flat on the cutting board. **Cut** the onion crosswise into semicircular slices. Then **chop** the slices into small pieces. Repeat with the other half. Set aside.

5. **Crack** the eggs into a small bowl. **Mix** with a fork until lightly whisked.

6. Use a grater to **grate** the mozzarella cheese. Set aside in a small bowl.

7. **Add** vegetable oil to the frying pan. Turn the burner under the pan on medium. **Add** the onions, peppers, and garlic. Cook for 5 minutes. **Add** the meat to the pan. Use a spatula to **stir**. Cook until meat is done. It should be completely browned, without any pink spots.

8. Ask an adult to **drain** off the extra oil or liquid from the pan into the sink or trash can. Then **stir** in the pasta sauce.

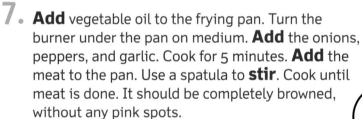

9. **Add** water to the saucepan and **cover**. Turn burner under the saucepan on high. Heat until water boils. **Add** pasta, stirring with a wooden spoon until it is all under water. Cook for 8 to 10 minutes, or follow the directions on the package. When it is done, ask an adult to **drain** the pasta into a colander in the sink.

10. Put the warm spaghetti into a large bowl. **Add** 1 tablespoon butter, Parmesan cheese, and eggs. **Mix** well with a large spoon. **Pour** the spaghetti mixture into the pie pan. **Press** the mixture into the bottom and up the sides of the pan to form a crust.

11. Use a spoon to **spread** the ricotta cheese on top of the spaghetti crust. Then spread on the meat and sauce mixture.

12. Use oven mitts to **place** the pie pan into the oven. **Bake** for 30 minutes. Use oven mitts to take the pan out of the oven. **Sprinkle** with mozzarella cheese. Let cheese melt, then cut the pie into slices and serve.

TRY THIS!

You can make this dish without meat. You can also use **tofu** instead of the ground beef or turkey. To cook the tofu, crumble it into the frying pan and cook it with the **onions** and **garlic**.

serves 4

preparation time: 20 minutes
cooking time: 0 minutes

ingredients:
1 medium head of cabbage
    (or 1 pound pre-chopped
    coleslaw mix)
½ red or green pepper
1 medium carrot
1 tablespoon vinegar
2 tablespoons peanut butter
2 tablespoons vegetable oil
2 tablespoons soy sauce
1 teaspoon packed brown
    sugar
1 package ramen noodles
    (any flavor)
½ cup peanuts

equipment:
cutting board
knife
grater
measuring cup—½ cup
medium bowl
measuring spoons
fork or spoon
large bowl
tongs or 2 large spoons

Peanutty Slaw

This salad has an extra crunch from uncooked noodles!
Give this peanutty recipe a try.

1. If you are cutting your own cabbage, **wash** the head of cabbage under cool water. Remove any leaves on the outside that are wilted. Use a knife and a cutting board to cut the cabbage. First, **cut** the cabbage in half. Then lay one of the halves flat on the cutting board. **Slice** the cabbage half into thin strips. **Chop** the strips into small pieces. Repeat with the other half. Measure out 4 cups. Set aside.

2. **Wash** the red or green pepper and the carrot under cool water. Use the knife and the cutting board to cut the vegetables. To cut the pepper, **cut** around the stem. Then cut the green pepper in half and remove the seeds. Discard the stem and the seeds. **Chop** half of the green pepper to make about ½ cup. Set aside. Save the other half of the pepper for another time.

3. **Grate** the carrot using the grater, discarding the stems. Grate enough to measure ½ cup and set aside.

4. In a medium bowl, **add** the vinegar, peanut butter, vegetable oil, soy sauce, and brown sugar. (To measure the brown sugar, be sure to pack it tightly into the measuring spoon.) **Mix** well with a fork or a spoon.

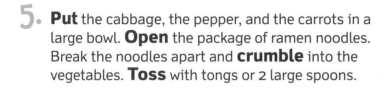

5. **Put** the cabbage, the pepper, and the carrots in a large bowl. **Open** the package of ramen noodles. Break the noodles apart and **crumble** into the vegetables. **Toss** with tongs or 2 large spoons.

6. **Pour** the peanut butter mixture on top of the vegetables. **Toss** with tongs or large spoons. **Sprinkle** the peanuts on top.

TRY THIS!

You can make this dish without the peanuts and peanut butter. Replace peanut butter with **almond** or **sunflower butter**, or just leave it out. Instead of peanuts, sprinkle **sesame seeds** or **sunflower seeds** on top. For extra flavor, you can also try adding ½ teaspoon of powdered or fresh, grated **ginger** in step 4.

serves 4 to 6

preparation time: 45 minutes
(includes cooking rice)
cooking time: 10 minutes

ingredients:

1 cup brown rice
2 cups water
2 green onions
1 medium carrot
2 eggs
2 tablespoon vegetable oil
1 cup frozen peas
2 tablespoons soy sauce

equipment:

measuring cups—½ cup, 1 cup
liquid measuring cup
medium saucepan
2 forks
knife
cutting board
grater
small bowl
large frying pan or wok
measuring spoons
spatula

Fantastic Fried Rice

Make your own delicious fried rice. This version uses brown rice, which takes a little longer to cook than white rice. Brown rice is healthier because it includes more whole-grain goodness.

1. **Measure** the rice and place it in saucepan. **Add** 2 cups water to the rice. **Cover** the pan. Turn the burner under the saucepan on high and cook until the water boils. Then turn down the heat to low. **Simmer** for 45 minutes, or until the rice has soaked up all the water. To see if the rice is done, lift the lid and stick a spoon or fork down to the bottom of the saucepan. If there is liquid at the bottom, the rice is not done yet. Cover the pan and cook for 2 to 3 more minutes. (Do not check the rice too often though. It does not cook as well if you keep lifting the lid.)

2. When the rice is done, turn off the heat, remove the lid, and **fluff** it with a fork.

3. While the rice is cooking, **wash** the green onions under cool water. Use the knife and the cutting board to cut the green onions. First, **cut** off the roots and discard. Remove any dry or wilted green parts. Then **slice** the onions into small pieces about ½ inch long. You can use both the white and green parts of the onion.

4. Use a grater to **grate** the carrot. Discard the stems. Grate enough to measure about ½ cup. Set aside the grated carrot in a small bowl.

5. **Crack** the eggs into a small bowl. **Whisk** lightly with a clean fork.

6. **Place** a large frying pan or wok on the stove. **Add** the vegetable oil and turn the burner under the pan on medium-high. Wait about 1 minute for the oil to get hot. **Add** the eggs. Let them cook for about 30 seconds until they begin to set. Then use the spatula to **stir** the eggs and **flip** them over. Keep stirring and flipping the eggs until they are cooked on all sides. They should be firm, not wet or gooey.

7. **Add** the rice, frozen peas, and carrots. **Stir** the ingredients together with the spatula. **Add** the soy sauce and mix well. Cook for about 5 minutes, stirring often. Turn off the heat. **Add** the green onions and mix one more time. Serve.

serves 4

preparation time: 15 minutes
cooking time: 35 to 40 minutes

ingredients:

1 10-ounce can condensed cream
   of broccoli soup
1½ cups water
¾ cup white rice
1 stalk broccoli (or 1 cup frozen
   broccoli)
1 tablespoon vegetable oil
4 chicken breasts
dash of pepper

equipment:

can opener
medium bowl
liquid measuring cup
knife
cutting board
measuring spoons
9 x 13-inch baking pan
plastic wrap (optional)
oven mitts

Chicken Broccoli Rice Bake

Your family will be impressed with this delicious and satisfying meal. It's easy to make!

1. **Preheat** the oven to 350°F.

2. Use a can opener to **open** the soup can. **Pour** the soup into a medium bowl. **Add** the water and stir.

3. **Add** the rice to the bowl and **mix**.

4. If you are using fresh broccoli, **wash** it under cool water. Use a knife and a cutting board to cut the broccoli. **Cut** off the bottom of the stem and discard. Cut the rest of the stem into large circular chunks. Then cut the broccoli tops lengthwise into several large pieces. Cut enough to make about 1 cup.

5. **Pour** the vegetable oil in the baking pan. **Rub** the oil around with your (clean) hands or a piece of plastic wrap to coat the whole pan.

6. **Place** the chicken breasts in the baking pan. Then wash your hands well with soap and water.

7. **Place** the broccoli pieces in the pan, spreading them evenly. Slowly **pour** the soup and the rice mixture over the chicken and the broccoli. **Sprinkle** with pepper.

8. Use oven mitts to **place** the baking pan into the oven. **Bake** for 35 to 40 minutes. Chicken should be cooked all the way through. To check if it is done, use oven mitts to take the pan out of the oven. Cut the largest piece of chicken in half. It should no longer be pink in the center. If the center is still pink, put the baking pan back in the oven for another 5 minutes. Serve.

serves 4

preparation time: 15 minutes
cooking time: 30 to 35 minutes

ingredients:

1 onion
2 tablespoons vegetable oil
1 teaspoon curry powder
¼ teaspoon cinnamon
½ teaspoon garlic powder
1 cup long-grain white rice
3 cups water
1½ cup frozen mixed vegetables
  (such as carrots, green beans,
  and broccoli)
2 tablespoons slivered almonds
⅓ cup raisins
¼ teaspoon salt (or to taste)

equipment:

knife
cutting board
measuring spoons
large saucepan
spatula
measuring cups—⅓ cup, ½ cup,
  1 cup
liquid measuring cup
fork

Quick Curry Rice

Try this recipe for a quick and simple supper.
The raisins add a sweet surprise to the mix.

1. Use the knife and cutting board to cut the onion. **Cut** off both ends of the onion. Set the onion on one of the flat parts you made by cutting it. Cut the onion in half. **Peel** off and discard the papery layers around the outside. Lay the onion half flat on the cutting board. **Cut** the onion crosswise into semicircular slices. Then **chop** the slices into small pieces. Repeat with the other half. Set aside.

2. **Measure** vegetable oil into a large saucepan. Turn the burner under the pan on medium-high. **Add** onion and cook for 5 minutes, stirring with a spatula or cooking spoon.

3. **Add** curry powder, cinnamon, and garlic powder to the onions. **Stir** for 1 minute.

4. **Add** the rice and **stir** for 1 minute.

5. **Add** water, frozen vegetables, almonds, raisins, and salt to the saucepan. **Cover** the pan. Bring the mixture to a boil. Then turn down the heat to low. **Simmer** for 20 to 25 minutes, or until the rice has soaked up all the water. To see if the rice is done, lift the lid and stick a spoon or fork down to the bottom of the saucepan. If there is water at the bottom, the rice is not done yet. Cover the pan and cook for 2 to 3 more minutes. (Do not check the rice too often though. It does not cook as well if you keep lifting the lid.)

6. **Fluff** the rice with a fork and serve.

serves 4

preparation time: 10 minutes
cooking time: 25 to 30 minutes

ingredients

1 medium onion
4 ounces (1 cup) cheddar or
   Monterey Jack cheese
1 tablespoon vegetable oil
¾ cup long-grain white rice
1 teaspoon ground cumin
½ teaspoon garlic salt
1½ cups (12 ounces) canned
   vegetable broth
1 cup frozen corn
1 can black beans
½ cup salsa

equipment:

knife
cutting board
grater
small bowl
measuring spoons
medium saucepan
spatula
measuring cups—¼ cup,
   ½ cup, 1 cup
can opener
liquid measuring cup
fork or spoon
microwave-safe bowl
oven mitts
colander

Cheesy Beans and Rice

Try this easy-to-make recipe for a delicious,
satisfying meal.

1. Use a knife and a cutting board to cut the onion. **Cut** off both ends of the onion. Set the onion on one of the flat parts you made by cutting it. Cut the onion in half. **Peel** off and discard the papery layers around the outside. Lay the onion half flat on the cutting board. **Cut** the onion crosswise into semicircular slices. Then **chop** the slices into small pieces. Repeat with the other half. Set aside.

2. Use a grater to **grate** the cheese into a small bowl.

3. **Measure** the vegetable oil into a medium saucepan. Turn the burner under the saucepan on high. Let the oil heat up for 1 minute. **Add** the onion. Cook for 5 minutes, stirring with a spatula.

TRY THIS!

Try some sliced avocado or fresh tomatoes on top. Or put this rice and bean mix in a tortilla and roll it up. (Heat the tortilla for 15 seconds in the microwave to warm it first.)

Turn the page for more Cheesy Beans and Rice

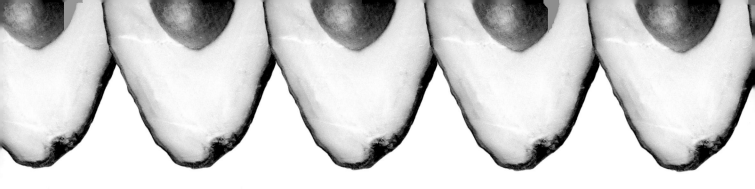

Cheesy Beans and Rice continued

4. **Add** the rice, cumin, and garlic salt to the saucepan. Cook for 1 minute.

5. Use a can opener to **open** the vegetable broth. Measure and **pour** it into the saucepan. **Cover** and bring to a boil. Turn the burner down to low. **Simmer** for 20 to 25 minutes, or until the rice has soaked up all the liquid. To see if the rice is done, lift the lid and stick a spoon or a fork down to the bottom of the saucepan. If there is broth at the bottom, the rice is not done yet. Cover the pan and cook for 2 to 3 more minutes. (Do not check the rice too often though. It does not cook as well if you keep lifting the lid.)

6. **Put** the frozen corn in a microwave-safe bowl and place it in the microwave. Cook on high for 1 to 2 minutes, until it is warm. Use oven mitts to take the bowl out of the microwave.

7. Use the can opener to **open** the black beans. Put a colander in the sink and **pour** the beans into the colander to drain the liquid.

8. **Add** the corn and beans to the cooked rice mixture. **Put** the cheese and salsa on top. Serve.

SPECIAL INGREDIENTS

avocado: a large, egg-shaped fruit with dark green bumpy or smooth skin, bright green flesh, and a large pit. Avocados can be found in the produce section of grocery stores.

bean sprouts: also called mung bean sprouts. These are bigger sprouts than the sprouts often used in sandwiches. (Those are alfalfa sprouts.) You can usually find bean sprouts in the grocery store's produce section.

broth or stock: the liquid part of a soup is called broth or stock. Look for it in the soup section of a grocery store. It comes in cans, cartons, and small jars. (Read the directions for use.)

cabbage: thick, crisp leaves that can be eaten raw or cooked. You can buy it as an uncut head of cabbage or pre-shredded in a bag. Look for it in the produce section of your grocery store.

cumin: a spice used in many types of cooking. Look for ground cumin in the spice aisle of the grocery store.

curry powder: a spice made from a mix of Indian spices, including turmeric, cumin, ginger, coriander, and cloves. Look for curry in the spice aisle of the grocery store.

pasta sauce: a jarred tomato sauce used for spaghetti and other pasta dishes. It can be found in the pasta aisle of the grocery store.

ramen noodles: thin, curvy noodles often used in Asian soups or crumbled raw over salads. Ramen noodles come in small, rectangular packages. You can find them in the soup aisle of most grocery stores or in Asian grocery stores.

rice noodles: noodles made from rice. Rice noodles are usually dry, like other pasta, and need to be cooked in water. If you don't find them in the pasta aisle of the grocery store, try the Asian section. You can also find rice noodles at an Asian grocery store.

ricotta cheese: a thick, creamy dairy product. You can find ricotta cheese near cottage cheese in the dairy section of the grocery store.

salsa: a sauce that may contain tomatoes, hot peppers, garlic, and herbs. It is often used to flavor Mexican dishes and can be found near the chips in the snack food aisle of the grocery store.

soy sauce: a salty sauce often used in Chinese and Japanese dishes. Look for it in the ethnic foods section of most grocery stores.

FURTHER READING AND WEBSITES

ChooseMyPlate.gov
http://www.choosemyplate.gov/children
-over-five.html
Download coloring pages, play an interactive computer game, and get lots of nutrition information at this U.S. Department of Agriculture website.

Dodge, Abigail Johnson, *Around the World Cookbook*, New York: DK Publishing, 2008. Check out these recipes from around the world, including some rice and noodle dishes.

Farmers Markets Search
http://apps.ams.usda.gov/FarmersMarkets/
Visit this site to find a farmers' market near you!

Feeding the Hungry with Rice
http://freerice.com
You can help people who can't afford to buy enough food to eat. Answer the quiz questions on this Web page. When you get the answers right, the World Food Programme will donate rice to people in need.

Food Activities
http://pbskids.org/lunchlab/#
Visit this Web page for fun games, videos, and quizzes all about food.

Food Games and Recipes
http://www.bam.gov/sub_foodnutrition
/index.html
Have fun while learning about nutrition!

Recipes
http://www.sproutonline.com/crafts-and
-recipes/recipes
Find more fun and easy recipes for kids at this site.

INDEX